Lerner SPORTS

MEXICO NATIONAL SOCCER TEAMS

ULTIMATE FAN GUIDE

KEITH ELLIOT GREENBERG

Lerner Publications ◆ Minneapolis

Lerner Publications Company
An imprint of Lerner Publishing Group, Inc.
241 First Avenue North
Minneapolis, MN 55401 USA

For reading levels and more information, look up this title at www.lernerbooks.com.

Main body text set in Aptifer Slab LT Pro.
Typeface provided by Linotype AG.

Editor: Evan Villas **Designer:** Viet Chu **Photo Editor:** Elena Mai

Library of Congress Cataloging-in-Publication Data

Names: Greenberg, Keith Elliot, 1959– author
Title: Mexico national soccer teams : ultimate fan guide / Keith Elliot Greenberg.
Description: Minneapolis : Lerner Publications, [2026] | Series: Lerner sports. World Cup fan guides | Includes bibliographical references and index. | Audience: Ages 7–11 | Audience: Grades 2–3 | Summary: "The Mexico national soccer teams have storied histories. And with talented men, powerhouse women, and a passionate fanbase, the future looks bright. Readers will learn the history and great moments of these teams"—Provided by publisher.
Identifiers: LCCN 2025011911 (print) | LCCN 2025011912 (ebook) | ISBN 9798765689356 lib. bdg | ISBN 9798348029272 pbk | ISBN 9798765698501 epub
Subjects: LCSH: Soccer players—Mexico—History | Soccer teams—Mexico—History
Classification: LCC GV944.M6 G74 2026 (print) | LCC GV944.M6 (ebook) | DDC 796.334/660972—dc23/eng/20250717

LC record available at https://lccn.loc.gov/2025011911
LC ebook record available at https://lccn.loc.gov/2025011912

Manufactured in the United States of America
1-1012733-54803-8/4/2025

TABLE OF CONTENTS

Oribe Peralta celebrates during the 2012 Olympic men's soccer final.

INTRODUCTION

GOING FOR THE GOLD

The stakes were high for Mexico. No men's soccer team from North America had won an Olympic gold medal in more than 100 years. Now, more than 86,000 fans were in London, England, watching Mexico's national team compete in the 2012 Olympic final against Brazil.

Only 29 seconds into the match, Mexico's Oribe Peralta kicked the ball into the net. At the time, it was the fastest goal in Olympic history. In the 75th minute, Peralta scored again.

Brazil managed to score late in the game. But Mexico stepped up its defense. Even though Brazil had a strong team, its players were unable to score another goal. Mexico won the gold medal!

Every four years, fans sing and chant for Mexico to win another Olympic gold medal. Mexico also competes in the World Cup every four years. Every two years, fans cheer as the men's and women's teams compete for glory in the CONCACAF Gold Cup tournament.

FAST FACTS

Mexico's men's team has won the CONCACAF Gold Cup 10 times.

Andrés Guardado appeared in five Men's World Cups for Mexico between 2006 and 2022.

Mexico qualified for its first Women's World Cup in 1999.

Goalkeeper Cecilia Santiago competed in the 2011 Women's World Cup when she was only 16 years old.

Mexico's men's team celebrating after winning the 2025 CONCACAF Gold Cup

CONCACAF teams come from North and Central America and the Caribbean. As of 2025, Mexico's men have won 10 CONCACAF Gold Cup titles. The team has also reached the World Cup quarterfinals three times.

Mexico's women's team has qualified for the World Cup three times. The Olympics have been more challenging.

Even so, the women's team has qualified for the tournament three times.

In 2024, it was announced that the 2026 Men's World Cup games would be held in North America. The locations included three Mexican cities. The decision had Mexico's soccer fans predicting great days ahead.

Mexico's women's team celebrates after a goal during a 2024 U-20 Women's World Cup match.

Isidoro Sota leaps for the ball during a Men's World Cup match in 1930.

CHAPTER 1

AGE OF HIGH HOPES

Immigrants from England introduced soccer to Mexico in the late 1800s. By 1923, Mexico had a men's national team. That team played in the 1928 Olympics. They also competed in the first ever Men's World Cup in 1930. They lost 4–1 to France in the first round.

At 21 years old, Mexico's Antonio Carbajal was the youngest goalkeeper to play in the 1950 World Cup. He played in the tournament five different times. By the time his career ended, Carbajal was nicknamed Five Cups.

Antonio Carbajal makes a save during a 1966 World Cup match.

In 1963, the Costa Rican women's soccer team toured Mexico. Mexico was inspired and formed its own women's team. But they weren't provided with modern equipment or proper playing fields. Fans still mostly paid attention to the men's team.

The men's team won the CONCACAF championship in 1965. Three years later, they stunned the world by beating the powerful Brazil team in a friendly match. The hero of the game was Enrique Borja. He scored both goals in the 2–1 victory.

Enrique Borja playing in the 1966 Men's World Cup

Javier Fragoso (*left*) kicks the ball in the 1970 Men's World Cup match against the Soviet Union.

In 1970, Mexico hosted the Men's World Cup. The men's team did well for their home crowd. They beat El Salvador and Belgium and tied with the Soviet Union. They made it to the quarterfinals but were knocked out of the tournament by Italy.

In 1970, there was no official Women's World Cup. But there was a women's tournament in Italy with teams from seven nations. Mexico finished in third place. The next year, Mexico reached the finals, losing 3–0 to Denmark. More than 110,000 fans filled Azteca Stadium in Mexico City to watch the women compete.

The most impressive player on the field was Mexico's Alicia Vargas. Vargas spent her whole life playing soccer. She was often compared to Pelé, one of the greatest soccer players ever. Vargas inspired many young women around Mexico to start playing soccer.

Mexico's women's national team in 1971

BREAKING THE RULES

As a child, Alicia Vargas insisted on playing soccer even though her parents argued that the sport was only for boys.

Mexico hosted the Men's World Cup again in 1986. This time, the team beat Belgium, Iraq, and Bulgaria, and tied with Paraguay. In the quarterfinals, Mexico kept the game close against West Germany before losing 4–1 in a penalty kick shootout.

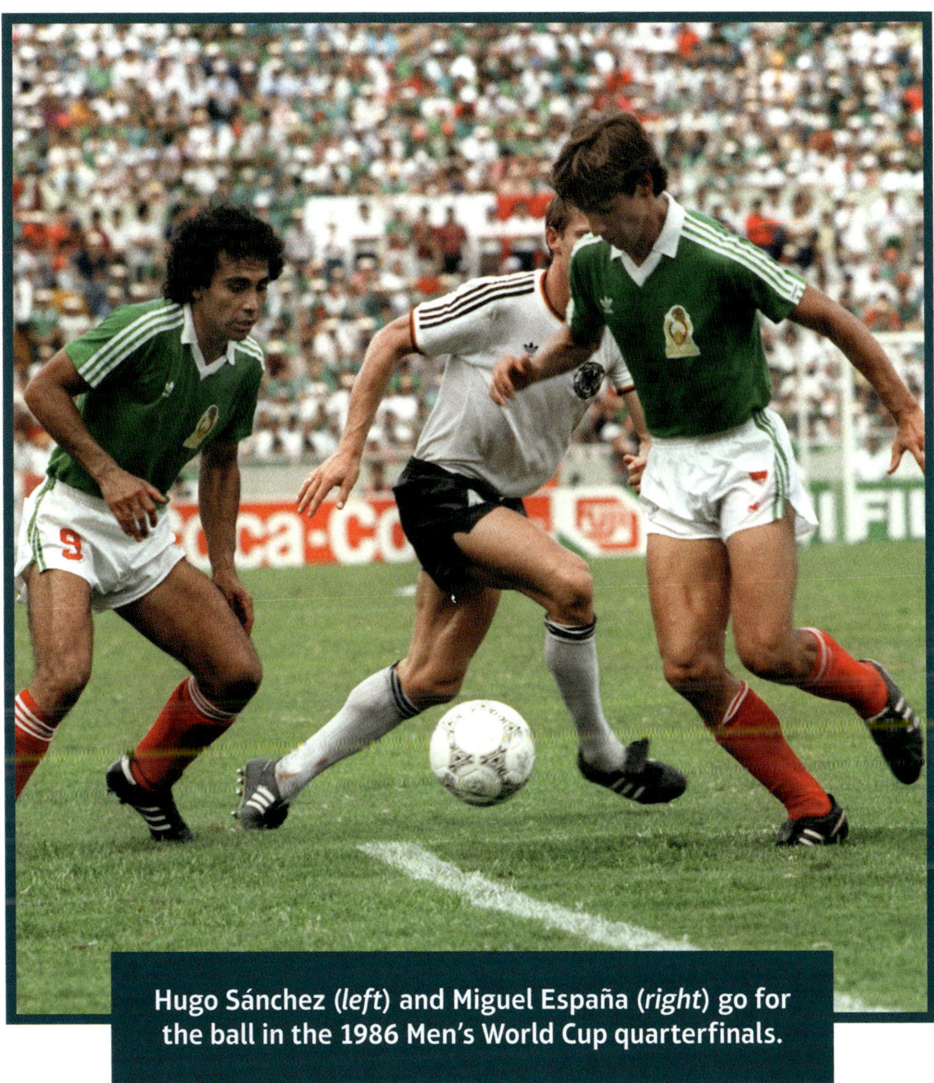

Hugo Sánchez (*left*) and Miguel España (*right*) go for the ball in the 1986 Men's World Cup quarterfinals.

The first Women's World Cup was held in 1991. Although the Mexican women's team did not qualify, they soon developed a fierce rivalry with the United States. Fans from these neighboring countries even argued about which players belonged on their teams.

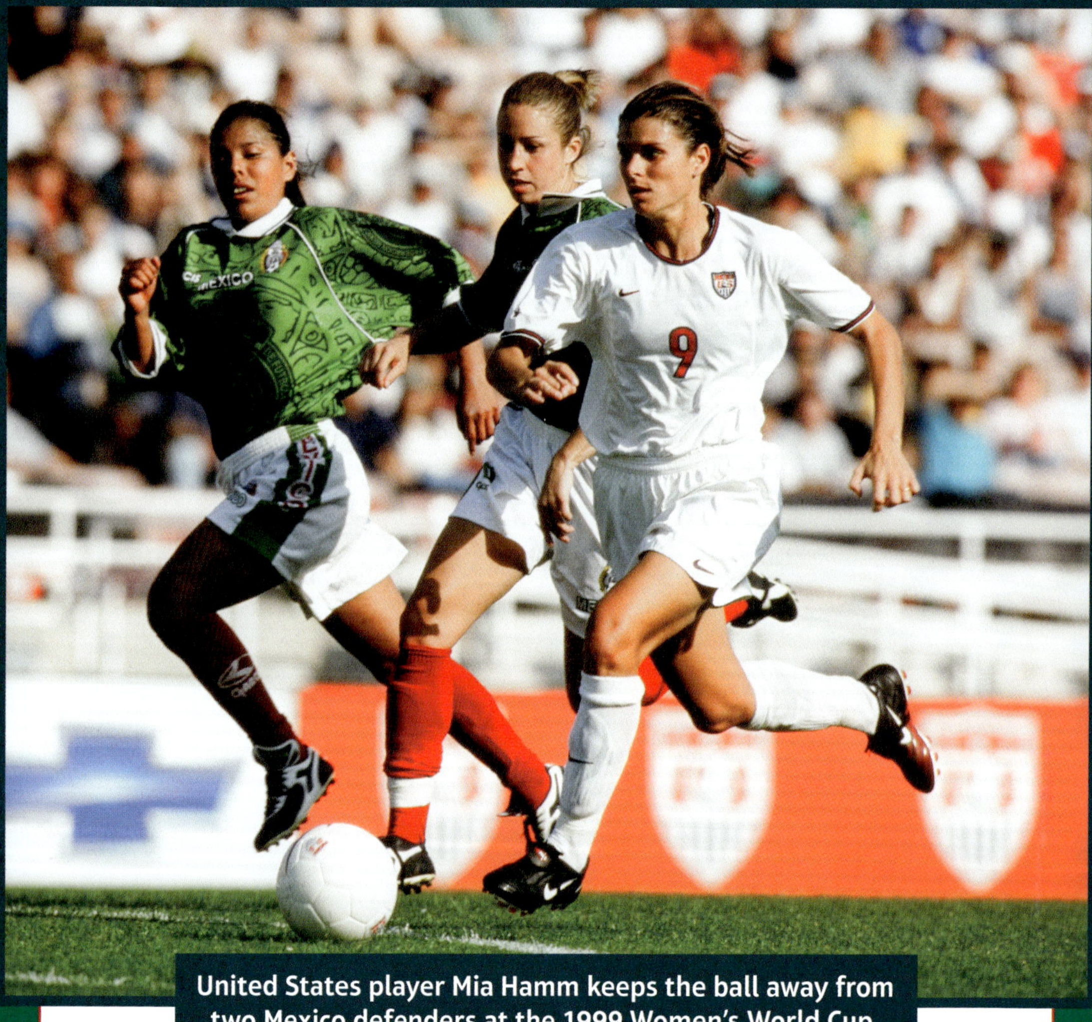

United States player Mia Hamm keeps the ball away from two Mexico defenders at the 1999 Women's World Cup.

Leonardo Cuéllar coaching the Mexican women's team during the 2015 Women's World Cup

CHAPTER 2

FIGHTING FOR VICTORY

Leonardo Cuéllar became the head soccer coach for the Mexican women in 1998. He kept the job for 18 years. No one else has coached either the Mexican men or women for so long. Cuéllar worked with many talented players during his time as coach.

Cecilia Santiago became the youngest goalkeeper to ever compete in the Women's World Cup in 2011. She was only 16 years old. Forward Maribel Domínguez's 75 career goals set a record for the team.

In 1999, Mexico qualified for the Women's World Cup. It was the first time that a Spanish-speaking country played in the tournament. Several of the Mexican players who competed had played on college teams in the United States.

Maribel Domínguez passes the ball during a 2016 match to qualify for the Olympics.

Andrés Guardado takes control of the ball during a match to qualify for the 2014 Men's World Cup.

The men's team started strong at the 2002 Men's World Cup. They beat Croatia and Ecuador early in the tournament. They almost lost to Italy in the next round. But a late header by Jared Borgetti led to a 1–1 tie and kept their hopes alive. They were knocked out in the next round by the United States.

Midfielder Andrés Guardado appeared in five World Cups for Mexico between 2006 and 2022. With 182 appearances, he has the most caps of any Mexican player. He scored 28 goals during his 16 years with the team.

Javier Hernández Balcázar controls the ball during a 2010 Men's World Cup match.

The Mexican men usually do well in CONCACAF competitions. In 2009, the team won its fifth Gold Cup. They shut out their rival United States 5–0 in the final.

Javier "Chicharito" Hernández Balcázar scored 52 goals during his time with Mexico's men's team. This is the most goals scored in the history of the team. These include goals scored at the 2010, 2014, and 2018 World Cups. In the 2011 CONCACAF Gold Cup tournament, Chicharito had seven goals.

Another great player of this time was Francisco Javier "Maza" Rodríguez. In addition to having a total of 100 caps for Mexico, he played in every match at the 2010 and 2014 World Cups. He was a key part of the team's defense.

Javier Rodríguez (*top*) goes for a header during the 2014 Men's World Cup match against Croatia.

The Mexican women came in second in the 2010 CONCACAF Gold Cup. Their success excited their fans. In the semifinal, the team beat their rival United States 2–0. It would be 14 years before Mexico would beat the United States again.

The Mexico women's national team at the 2024 CONCACAF Gold Cup semifinal

FAMILY TIES

Leonardo Cuéllar and his son, Christopher, have both coached for the Mexico women's national soccer team. Leonardo was the head coach from 1998 to 2016, while Christopher was the head coach from 2019 to 2020.

The United States' Alejandro Bedoya (*left*) defends against Mexico's Carlos Salcido during the 2011 CONCACAF Gold Cup championship.

Around this time, the attitude around women's soccer was changing in Mexico. Women's games were shown on Mexican television. With soccer programs being offered around the country, more girls than ever were taking up the sport.

Like the women, the men's team wanted to beat the Americans. They got their wish during the 2011 Gold Cup final when they defeated the United States in Los Angeles. It was the team's sixth Gold Cup win.

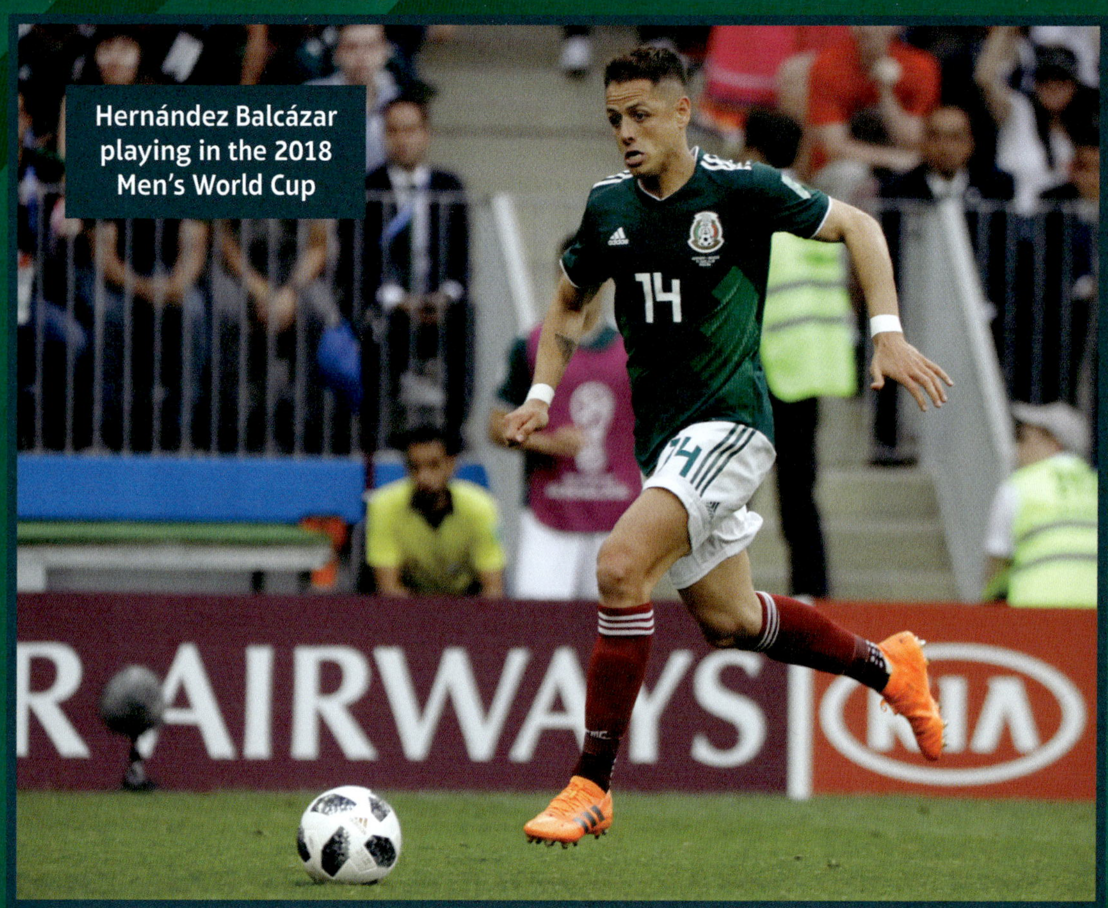

Hernández Balcázar playing in the 2018 Men's World Cup

During the 2018 Men's World Cup, Mexico beat defending champions Germany in the first round. More than 75,000 fans rushed to the center of Mexico City to celebrate. That year, Mexico made it to the tournament's Round of 16.

The next year was even better for fans of the men's team. In the 2019 Gold Cup, Mexico beat both Costa Rica and Haiti. Then they beat the United States 1–0 in Chicago in the final. They had just won the tournament for the eighth time.

Fans attend a viewing party of the 2022 Men's World Cup.

CHAPTER 3

FOR THE FLAG

Before games, Mexico fans dress in the three colors of the nation's flag: green, white, and red. A common outfit is a red shirt, white jacket, and green pants. Fans call the men's team *El Tri* and the women's *La Tri* after the country's three-colored flag.

The men's and women's teams both play home games at Azteca Stadium in Mexico City. It is one of the largest soccer stadiums in the world. More than 100,000 fans pack the building to cheer on their heroes.

Fans of Mexico who live in the United States sometimes call themselves Pancho Villa's Army. They are named after one of Mexico's historic leaders. The group has chapters all over the US. Matches at the Rose Bowl in California have attracted more than 90,000 fans of the teams.

Mexico national soccer teams play at Estadio Azteca, or Azteca Stadium.

Goalkeeper Guillermo Ochoa leaps for the ball during the 2023 CONCACAF Gold Cup final.

At the 2022 World Cup, the men's team didn't make it past the opening round. After this defeat, they were eager to prove themselves in the 2023 Gold Cup. They beat Panama 1–0 in the final to take home their ninth Gold Cup trophy. In 2025, Mexico beat the United States 2–1 to win their 10th Gold Cup.

DEEP IN THE HEART OF TEXAS

AT&T Stadium in Dallas has been called "the second home" of Mexico's men's soccer team. The team has played there many times because of a partnership with the Dallas Cowboys, FC Dallas, and the Dallas Sports Commission.

Mayra Pelayo (*left*) and Lizbeth Ovalle celebrate Ovalle's goal at the 2024 CONCACAF Gold Cup.

Pedro López became the head coach of the women's team in 2022. During the 2024 Gold Cup competition, the team beat the United States after Lizbeth Ovalle and Mayra Pelayo scored goals. This pair, along with María Sánchez and captain Rebeca Bernal, has given fans hope for the future of the team.

Javier Aguirre became the men's coach for the third time in 2024. He heads a team that includes stars such as goalkeeper Guillermo Ochoa and striker Raúl Jiménez. As a player, Aguirre played in the 1986 World Cup. He was also the coach when Mexico played in the World Cup in 2002 and 2010.

The 2026 Men's World Cup will take place in Mexico City, Guadalajara, and Monterrey, as well as other North American cities. Some fans are certain that the time has come for Mexico to finally win the top prize. The women's team also promises to make supporters proud during the 2027 Women's World Cup in Brazil. Win or lose, followers will keep singing, chanting, and cheering for their teams' victories.

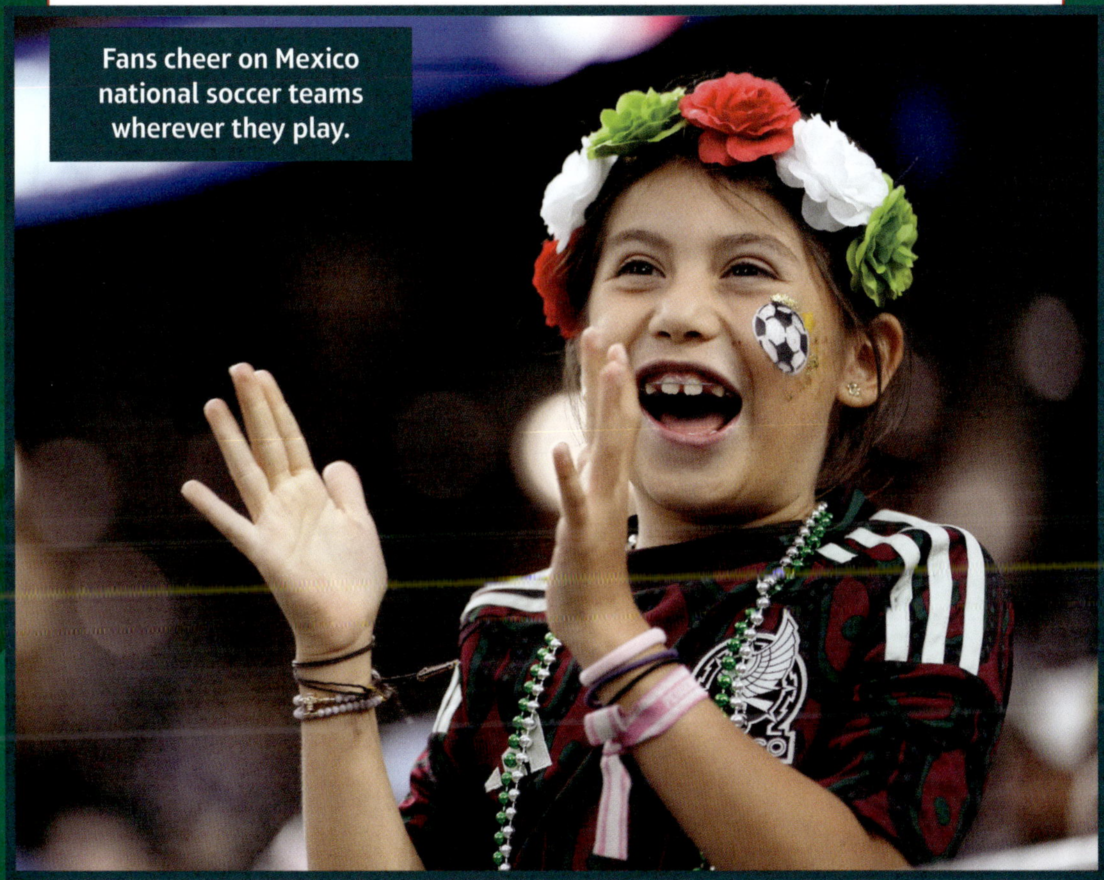

Fans cheer on Mexico national soccer teams wherever they play.

MEXICO MEN'S TEAM TIMELINE

1923 Mexico forms a national men's soccer team.

1928 Mexico competes in the Olympics for the first time.

1930 The team plays in the first-ever World Cup game, losing to France 4–1.

1970 Mexico hosts the World Cup and reaches the quarterfinals.

1986 Mexico hosts the World Cup again, reaching the quarterfinals once more.

1993 Mexico wins its first CONCACAF Gold Cup.

2012 The team wins the gold medal in soccer at the Olympics in London.

2023 The team wins the CONCACAF Gold Cup for the ninth time.

2025 Mexico wins the CONCACAF Gold Cup for the 10th time.

2026 Mexico hosts the World Cup with the United States and Canada.

MEXICO WOMEN'S TEAM TIMELINE

1963 Mexico forms a women's national soccer team.

1970 Mexico takes third place in an international tournament considered part of the Women's World Cup tradition.

1971 The team reaches the finals of the international tournament.

Alicia Vargas builds her reputation as one of the world's best soccer players.

1998 Leonardo Cuéllar begins his 18-year run as the Mexican women's coach.

1999 Mexico qualifies for its first Women's World Cup.

2010 Mexico beats the United States in the CONCACAF Gold Cup semifinal.

The team takes second place in the Gold Cup tournament.

2019 Leonardo Cuéllar's son, Christopher, becomes the women's head coach.

2024 Mexico beats the United States in a Gold Cup game for the first time in 14 years.

GLOSSARY

cap: an appearance for a country's national team

CONCACAF: a group that oversees soccer in North American, Central American, and Caribbean nations

friendly: a game that doesn't take place in a tournament or count for official standings

Gold Cup: a CONCACAF tournament held every two years

header: when a player uses their head to strike the ball

immigrant: someone who moves to a new country

penalty kick: a free kick at the goal allowed for certain fouls or to decide the winner of some games

quarterfinal: the round played by the final eight teams in a tournament.

Round of 16: the round of a tournament featuring 16 teams

semifinal: the round played by the final four teams in a tournament